Paint along with
NANCY KOMINSKY
Oil painting made easy

COLLINS
Glasgow & London

First published 1974
Published by William Collins Sons & Co. Ltd., Glasgow and London

Designed and edited by Youé & Spooner Ltd.

© Sportontv 1974
Filmset by Trade Spools, Frome, Somerset
Printed in Great Britain by John Bartholomew & Son Ltd, Edinburgh
ISBN 0 00 411830 8

For all the paintings in this book Nancy Kominsky has used Rowney Georgian Oil Colours which she has found to be most suitable for her purposes. They are permanent and their consistency is incomparable for palette knife painting.

Contents

Introduction

If you have always wanted to paint and have never known where to start, or you have been painting for a while and hanging your paintings in the cupboard, then this is the book for you.

Most likely you have become confused and frustrated by the non-teaching teachers who tell you to "Paint what you feel". As a matter of fact, there was a teacher (who shall be nameless) who had his students painting circles until "something happened". I understand they are still painting circles.

As a result of having gone all through this myself, I have evolved a commonsense theory for painting, based on discipline right from the start. After all, there are rules for everything we do in life: driving, music, dancing and so on.

When I was learning to paint, drawing was stressed. Consequently, when I actually began to paint, it was as though I had never had a lesson. The paintings were tight and the colour muddy. It took me years to learn colour (mostly trial and error), and produce a fairly acceptable painting. For too much drawing inhibits painting. In a painting, it is colour that is important. When you have good tonal values, very little drawing is required and should be reduced to basic essentials.

Starting with this premise, I devised a unique and instantly productive system of learning to paint, for you, the absolute beginner. All the guesswork has been removed in mixing colour, by colour formulas in exact amounts, like baking a cake. Just follow the recipe.

You will notice in painting the pictures in this book (which you have seen on the Paint Along With Nancy Kominsky television series), how this stroke-by-stroke methodical approach to painting is not only beautifully logical and painless, but I promise you a painting on your very first attempt.

Painting materials

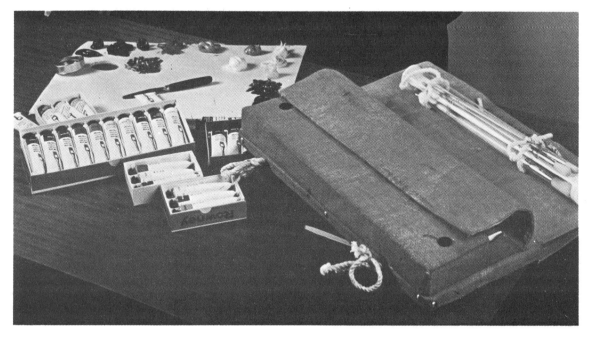

The following colours and other required painting materials can be purchased in a complete Nancy Kominsky Paint Along Kit. However, you can buy them separately, if you wish, from most art material stockists. I have kept the list to the absolute minimum for economical reasons.

No substitutions of colours should be made, otherwise your colour mixes will not turn out the same as mine.

PAINTS

Lemon Yellow
Yellow Ochre
Naples Yellow
Cadmium Yellow deep
Cadmium Orange deep
Vermilion (red)
Alizarin Crimson
Viridian (green)
French Ultramarine (blue)
Burnt Umber
Extra large tube of Zinc or Flake White

PALETTE KNIVES

Offset knife, for painting
Straight knife, for mixing colour (optional)

BRUSHES

1 No. 10, 11 or 12 flat hog brush, for umber wash
1 No. 6 round sable brush, for drawing

OTHER MATERIALS

Turpentine, or white spirit if you do not like the smell of turpentine
Single tin dipper for turpentine or white spirit (medium)
Large square wooden palette or tear-off palette pad
Toilet tissue which is disposable and therefore more practical and cleaner than cloths
Plastic litter bag
Polythene or tin foil. Use either of these to cover your left-over paint on the palette, pop it into the fridge and your paint will keep indefinitely
Artists' clear picture varnish — no hurry for this. Paintings should not be varnished in under six months' drying time
Canvas, canvas board, or hardboard which is adequate and less expensive
Easel — whatever available and sturdy

WORK AREA

The ideal would be a room facing north but you will probably end up in a corner of any room that is spare, using electric light. It is really unimportant where you work, as long as you have the space to move and are comfortable. After all, Michelangelo painted on his back with a candle strapped to his head for four years and you cannot do better than the Sistine Chapel!

Measurements for colour formulas

In a painting, colour is most important — even more than the drawing. At the risk of sounding unartistic and homey, I have broken down colour into almost exact amounts, rather like a recipe. I am going to use spoons for measuring, as this helps to keep amounts uniform. Of course, this gives me qualms, as I have visions of paint actually being measured out with spoons. Don't. Just gauge it by eye. This naturally means the amounts are *not* level.

The illustration below shows the amounts used in colour mixtures.

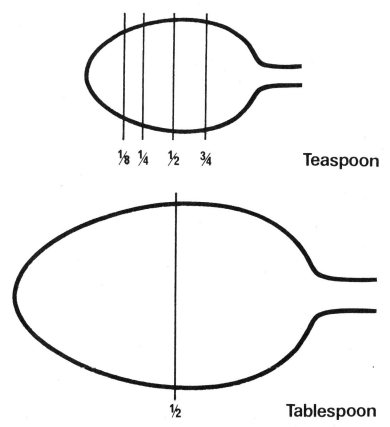

⅛ ¼ ½ ¾   **Teaspoon**

½   **Tablespoon**

These amounts are geared mostly for knife painting which requires more paint, and ensure having the adequate amount of paint for each area in the painting.

Colour formulas in this series are interchangeable. For example, the burnt orange tones for the background of Sunflowers on page 13 will be the same colour formula as that used for the bowl in Pears on page 35. Also, the tones of green are used in 12 paintings.

Paint the areas of the painting in the logical order presented.

Painting procedures

1 Your first step is to cover the canvas with an umber wash. This gives the painting a richer colour and also allows you to wipe off the drawing if you make a mistake. To make the umber wash, squeeze out $\frac{1}{2}$ teaspoon burnt umber. Dip your No. 10, 11 or 12 flat brush into the turpentine or white spirit (it should not be dripping), and then into the burnt umber on the palette, pulling some aside to make a light, rather thin wash. Cover the canvas with the wash, taking care not to make it too dark or runny. Wipe the excess moisture with tissue but leave the canvas damp.

2 For the sectioning on the canvas use the No. 6 round sable brush. Dip the brush in the umber wash. If your canvas is to be used vertically, draw three vertical lines equally spaced and five horizontal lines. If your canvas is to be used horizontally, section it off with five equally spaced vertical lines and three horizontal lines (see the vertical drawing on page 12 and the horizontal drawing on page 16).

3 Put in the drawing reduced to simple form and the shading with the same umber wash and the No. 6 round sable brush. Use tissue to erase, if necessary.

4 Set up your palette as shown in the photograph and key illustration opposite, using about a teaspoonful of each colour and mixing the aqua, purple and mixed green as instructed. The palette should be set up the same way each time and a copy of the set-up kept in the kit.

5 Be accurate when mixing your colours. You will find that the colour mixtures will vary slightly from the colour formulas but this is normal. Just make sure that you keep the correct tonal values.

6 Keep your paint on your palette clean while working, by cleaning your knife before going from one colour to another.

7 Dabbling and stippling are two techniques you will find used a great deal in this book. To stipple colour on the canvas, put a small amount of paint on the tip of your knife or brush and cover the area required with short, sharp strokes to give a rough, raised texture. For dabbling, use a little more paint and, with the flat part of the top of the knife or brush, dab short strokes on the required area.

8 Six months after you have completed your painting, dust it off with a dry, soft paint brush and apply the clear varnish lightly: Lay the painting flat until dry — this will take about an hour.

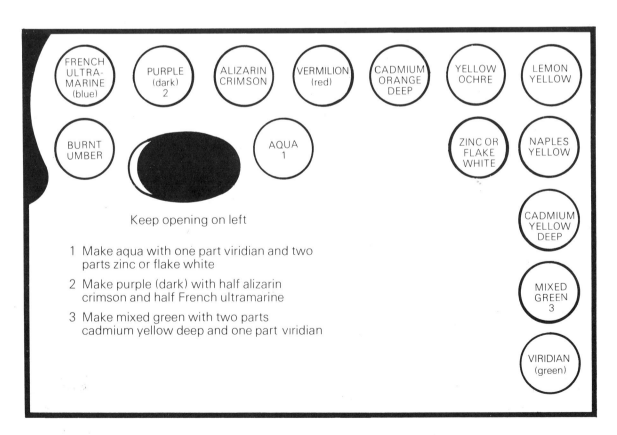

| FRENCH ULTRA-MARINE (blue) | PURPLE (dark) 2 | ALIZARIN CRIMSON | VERMILION (red) | CADMIUM ORANGE DEEP | YELLOW OCHRE | LEMON YELLOW |

| BURNT UMBER | | AQUA 1 | | | ZINC OR FLAKE WHITE | NAPLES YELLOW |

CADMIUM YELLOW DEEP

MIXED GREEN 3

VIRIDIAN (green)

Keep opening on left

1 Make aqua with one part viridian and two parts zinc or flake white

2 Make purple (dark) with half alizarin crimson and half French ultramarine

3 Make mixed green with two parts cadmium yellow deep and one part viridian

Lesson 1
Sunflowers

Florals are best at the beginning. Keep the painting simple.

THE DRAWING
1 Use canvas board or canvas, 14 inches by 18 inches vertically.
2 Study the drawing and painting on pages 12 and 13.
3 Arrange the palette according to the palette layout on the previous page.
4 Use the No. 10, 11 or 12 flat brush to stain the canvas with a wash of burnt umber and white spirit, as described in Step 1 on page 8. Wipe with toilet tissue.
5 With the No. 6 round brush and umber wash put in the grid lines and simple drawing as indicated on page 12.
6 The light is coming from the left and, as the flowers are cupped, it is hitting the petals on the opposite side. So lightly shade in the areas on the left half of the flowers using the same umber wash.
7 Clean your brushes in the medium (turpentine or white spirit).

THE PAINTING
Always mix paints with the straight knife.

BACKGROUND(always painted in first)

Colour formula
Tones of burnt orange

light   medium   dark

Medium tone
1 tablespoon orange
$\frac{1}{2}$ teaspoon vermilion
$\frac{1}{4}$ teaspoon purple
Mix and separate into three parts, one small ($\frac{1}{2}$ teaspoon) and two equal parts.
First part ($\frac{1}{2}$ teaspoon) for light tone
add $\frac{1}{2}$ teaspoon white
$\frac{1}{2}$ teaspoon orange

Second part for medium tone: do not touch

Third part for dark tone
add $\frac{1}{4}$ teaspoon purple
$\frac{1}{4}$ teaspoon alizarin crimson

Clean your knife.

Let's paint
Use offset knife, held lightly.

1 Study the background in the painting on page 13.
2 Paint the background in thirds of light, medium and dark tones, the dark tones first, starting on the right.
3 Blend the tones slightly and go around the flowers loosely. The knife will feel awkward at first.
4 Move left-over paint out of the mixing area and clean the palette.
5 It is best to leave the background to dry before putting in the flowers.

PETALS

Colours
Tones of yellow

lemon yellow   cadmium yellow deep   yellow ochre

light   medium   dark

The above colours are used from the palette and require no mixing.

1 Paint each petal on the left side of the flowers in the three different tones. Use yellow ochre at the base of each petal, cadmium yellow deep in the centre and lemon yellow on the tip.
2 For the petals on the right side of the flowers, use lemon yellow at the base of each petal, cadmium yellow deep in the centre and yellow ochre on the tip.

CENTRES

Colours

cadmium orange deep   alizarin crimson

light   dark

The above colours are used from the palette and require no mixing.

1 The pods should look raised and textured, so stipple on the alizarin crimson thickly.
2 Dabble the orange on the left for highlight and blend both colours lightly.
3 With purple from palette, outline unevenly on right side and bottom of pod for shadow.
4 Paint between petals lightly with purple from palette.

Lesson 1 continues on page 14

LEAVES, STEMS, BUD

Colour formula
Tones of green

light medium dark

Medium tone
1 tablespoon yellow ochre
½ teaspoon mixed green
¼ teaspoon vermilion
¼ teaspoon orange

Mix and separate into three parts, one small (½ teaspoon) and two equal parts.

First part (½ teaspoon) for light tone
add 1 teaspoon white
1 teaspoon lemon yellow

Second part for medium tone: do not touch

Third part for dark tone
add ¼ teaspoon purple
½ teaspoon mixed green

Clean your knife.

1 Because this is your first painting, use No. 6 round brush instead of the knife for this stage. With dark tone of green, lightly draw in stems, leaves and bud.
2 Put a line of dark tone down the centre of the leaves.
3 With offset knife, paint medium and dark tones of green on back half of leaves.
4 Paint light tone on front of leaves.
5 Paint stems mostly dark tone with some light tone near the base. Paint a little purple below flowers on the stems.
6 Paint bud light green tone on left, dark tone on right. Paint cadmium and lemon yellow peeping out of the bud.
7 Paint a few strokes of light green tone on left side of each flower centre.
8 Put in accents of aqua lightly where indicated in the painting — mostly in the shaded areas of the floral and background.

Clean palette, brushes and knives.

The Sunflowers are finished and beautiful. Remember, this is your first painting in the series. Relax — they will become easier as you paint along.

Lesson 2
Rocky Coast

No crashing waves — a calm sea is best for your first marine painting.

THE DRAWING
1 Use canvas board or canvas, 14 inches by 18 inches horizontally.
2 Study the drawing and painting on pages 16 and 17.
3 Arrange the palette according to the palette layout on page 9.
4 Prepare canvas as you did for Sunflowers, stained with umber wash and sectioned off with grid lines. (All canvases are prepared in the same way.) Always start any marine, landscape or street scene painting by placing a line for the horizon. The horizon in this painting is a little above the centre line. It does not cut the painting in half.
5 Using No. 6 round brush and umber wash, draw in mountains first. Study the placement on grid line carefully in the drawing. Do not draw any sharp uniform points, but keep the lines soft and undulating, and of varied heights.
6 Put in the rest of the drawing. Again, the rocks are softly rounded. Do not draw too many.
7 The light is coming from the left, so lightly shade in the areas on the right.
8 Clean your brushes in the medium (turpentine or white spirit).

THE PAINTING
Always mix paints with straight knife.

SKY (always paint in sky first)

Colour formula
Sky tones

light   medium   dark

Medium tone
1 tablespoon white
$\frac{1}{4}$ teaspoon blue
$\frac{1}{4}$ teaspoon aqua
$\frac{1}{4}$ teaspoon orange
Mix and separate into three parts, one small ($\frac{1}{2}$ teaspoon) and two equal parts.
First part ($\frac{1}{2}$ teaspoon) for light tone
add   1 teaspoon white
$\frac{1}{2}$ teaspoon Naples yellow

Second part for medium tone: do not touch

Third part for dark tone
add $\frac{1}{8}$ teaspoon blue
$\frac{1}{4}$ teaspoon aqua
$\frac{1}{4}$ teaspoon orange
$\frac{1}{8}$ teaspoon purple

Clean your knife.

In this painting, only the light and medium tones are used for the sky. The dark tone is used for the mountains.

Let's paint
Use offset knife, held lightly.

1 Study the sky in the painting on the previous page.
2 Paint the light tone around the top of the mountains and into part of the sky. Use the flat of the knife, as the point makes ridges.
3 Paint remaining sky with medium tone, dragging the colour from top of canvas down to mountains in a slanting stroke. Blend the tones but take care to retain the light tone around the mountains.

MOUNTAINS

Colour tone
to each of the medium and dark sky tones
add ⅛ teaspoon purple

1 Paint the right side of the mountains in the dark tone just mixed, then the left side in the medium tone just mixed. Use long, flowing strokes.
2 Clean knife, then lightly and carefully drag a bit of sky into the mountains to soften the line.

COASTLINE

Colour formula
Tones of green

    light   medium   dark

Refer to page 14 for tones of green and mix according to the directions. (The same tones of green are used in all the paintings in the book.)

1 Study the coastline in the painting on the previous page.
2 Paint the hill in front of the mountains alternately with dark green tone and purple from the palette. Take care with your strokes.
3 Continue with the dark green tone and purple on the right side and bottom of the canvas (foreground).
4 On this same foreground, stipple light green tone over the dark tone for grass and scrub.

ROCKS

Colour formula
Tones of beige

    light   medium   dark

Medium tone
1 teaspoon yellow ochre
$\frac{1}{8}$ teaspoon purple

Mix and separate into three parts, one small ($\frac{1}{2}$ teaspoon) and two equal parts.

First part ($\frac{1}{2}$ teaspoon) for light tone
add $\frac{3}{4}$ teaspoon white
      $\frac{1}{2}$ teaspoon cadmium yellow deep
      $\frac{1}{8}$ teaspoon orange

Second part for medium tone: do not touch

Third part for dark tone
add $\frac{1}{8}$ teaspoon purple
      touch of orange

Clean your knife.

1 Paint the bit of the beach at the foot of the hill on the right with medium and light tones.
2 Paint rocks with medium and dark tones on the right side, using downward strokes, slanted right.
3 Add some purple at the base of rocks for shadows.
4 Paint light tone in slanting strokes towards the left.
5 Blend dark green tone with purple around base of rocks.

WATER

Colour formula
Tones of blue

light   medium   dark

Medium tone
1 tablespoon white
$\frac{3}{4}$ teaspoon aqua
$\frac{1}{2}$ teaspoon blue
$\frac{1}{8}$ teaspoon orange
$\frac{1}{8}$ teaspoon mixed green

Mix and separate into three parts, one small ($\frac{1}{2}$ teaspoon) and two equal parts.

First part ($\frac{1}{2}$ teaspoon) for light tone
add $\frac{3}{4}$ teaspoon white
      $\frac{1}{2}$ teaspoon Naples yellow
      $\frac{1}{4}$ teaspoon aqua

Second part for medium tone: do not touch

Third part for dark tone
add $\frac{1}{2}$ teaspoon blue
      $\frac{3}{4}$ teaspoon aqua
      $\frac{1}{2}$ teaspoon orange

Clean your knife.

1 Study the painting on page 17.
2 With offset knife, paint strokes of dark blue tone at left side of canvas. The strokes should go straight across and be slightly dipped. Be careful that the water does not go up or down hill.
3 Start blending in medium tone, going between rocks and overlapping mountains a little.
4 Starting at rocks in the middle of the painting, blend in light tone.
5 Add an extra $\frac{1}{2}$ teaspoon white and $\frac{1}{4}$ teaspoon Naples yellow to light tone and use this colour for the shallow water around these rocks. Paint to shoreline.

FOAM

Colour tone
$\frac{3}{4}$ teaspoon white
$\frac{1}{4}$ teaspoon Naples yellow

1 Study the shoreline in the painting on page 17.
2 Dribble foam colour in the shape of the shoreline around rocks, etc., as shown in the painting.
3 Drag foam lightly with clean knife back over the water.

SEAGULLS, GRASSES
1 With tip of knife and purple from palette, paint in gulls as shown. Paint them very thin. No vultures or eagles, please!
2 Clean your knife and scratch in grasses between rocks in foreground, using upward strokes in wet paint. No colour is needed.

Clean palette, brushes and knives.

I am sure this painting was a little easier. Carry on and keep painting.

Lesson 3
Still Life

THE DRAWING

1 Use canvas board or canvas, 14 inches by 18 inches horizontally.
2 Study the drawing and painting on pages 22 and 23.
3 Arrange the palette according to the palette layout on page 9.
4 Prepare canvas as for the previous paintings, stained with umber wash and sectioned off.
5 Put in the drawing, using grids for correct placement. Draw vegetables, etc., through each other, as shown. This is to avoid distortion.
6 The light is coming from the left, so lightly shade in the right side of vegetables, etc., as indicated in the drawing.
7 Clean your brushes in the medium (turpentine or white spirit).

THE PAINTING

BACKGROUND

Colour formula
Tones of grey-blue

light   medium   dark

Medium tone
1 tablespoon white
$\frac{1}{4}$ teaspoon blue
$\frac{1}{2}$ teaspoon aqua
$\frac{3}{4}$ teaspoon orange

Mix and separate into three parts, one small ($\frac{1}{2}$ teaspoon) and two equal parts.

First part ($\frac{1}{2}$ teaspoon) for light tone
add   1 teaspoon white
$\frac{1}{2}$ teaspoon yellow ochre

Second part for medium tone: do not touch

Third part for dark tone
add $\frac{1}{4}$ teaspoon blue
$\frac{1}{2}$ teaspoon orange
$\frac{1}{8}$ teaspoon purple
$\frac{1}{2}$ teaspoon aqua

Clean your knife.

Let's paint

1 Study the painting on page 23.
2 Start painting with dark tone on the right of the background, then medium tone, and light tone on the left. Use long strokes, with flat of knife.
3 Using purple from palette, paint in foreground under the vegetables, etc. Then, with

the flat of knife, drag purple lightly in downward strokes for shadows and reflections. Scratch in a few strokes horizontally with a clean knife.

4 Stroke a little purple on right side of canvas.

JAR

Colours
Tones of yellow

lemon yellow   cadmium yellow deep   yellow ochre

light   medium   dark

The above colours are used from the palette and require no mixing.

1 Study the structure of the jar carefully.
2 Paint right side of jar with yellow ochre. Do not lose the form and stay within the lines of the drawing.
3 Paint cadmium yellow deep in the middle of the jar, then clean your knife.
4 Paint lemon yellow on the left, going around the lid carefully. Paint the stem of the knob yellow ochre and the top lemon yellow for highlight.
5 Outline the jar lightly with purple and work a little purple on right side, down to vegetables.

GREEN PEPPER

Colour formula
Tones of green

light   medium   dark

Refer to page 14 for tones of green and mix according to the directions.

1 Study the painting on the previous page.
2 Paint the pepper in three sections, adding highlights later.
3 Paint section on right with dark tone and the centre with medium tone.
4 Paint the second section with medium tone and the centre with light tone.
5 Paint the third section in the same way as the second section, with medium and light tones.
6 Stroke a little purple upwards on the pepper at the back of the parsley, and on right side of pepper.
7 Paint the stem in purple.

TOMATOES

cadmium orange deep   vermilion   alizarin crimson

light   medium   dark

The above colours are used from the palette and require no mixing.

1 Using round strokes, paint dark tone on right side and bottom of each tomato and around the stem area.
2 Paint medium tone in the centre of each tomato, using round strokes to maintain the form.
3 Paint light tone on the left side in the same strokes. Blend them slightly.
4 Paint a few short light and dark green strokes in the stem area, using the green tones mixed for the green pepper.

CARROTS

cadmium yellow deep   cadmium orange deep   alizarin crimson

light   medium   dark

The above colours are used from the palette and require no mixing.

1 Paint the bottom length of the carrots in the dark tone.
2 Paint medium tone on the length of each carrot, using half-round strokes.
3 Paint light tone on the top edge over the medium tone, taking care not to lose the medium tone.
4 Paint a few light and medium green tones for short stems on the carrot.

ONIONS

light   medium   dark

Refer to page 18 for tones of beige and mix according to the directions.

1 Study the painting on page 23.
2 Paint dark tone on the right side and bottom of the onions, using round strokes.

3 Paint medium tone in the middle.
4 Paint light tone on the left side of the onions.
5 Bring the dark tone and the light tone up to create a tassle effect at the top.
6 Paint pearl onions in the foreground in light tone of left-over background colour.

PARSLEY

Colour formula
Tones of green

light   medium   dark

Refer to page 14 for tones of green and mix according to the directions. These are the same tones as those used for the green pepper.

1 Using stippling stroke, paint the dark tone on the right side of all the parsley. Put some dark tone in the centre, too.
2 Stipple medium tone on the rest of all the parsley.
3 Stipple light tone on the left side, over the medium tone, and across the top of all the parsley.
4 Stipple a little purple in the parsley behind both tomatoes.

HIGHLIGHTS
For peppers, tomatoes, onion and stem of pepper.

Colour tone
$\frac{3}{4}$ teaspoon white
$\frac{1}{4}$ teaspoon Naples yellow

1 Paint a short curved blob in the shape of the vegetables on the left, where shown in the painting on page 23.
2 Paint a stroke of cadmium yellow deep on stem of pepper.

Clean palette, brushes and knives.

This was a busy painting but I am sure it was well worth all your efforts.

Lesson 4
Spring in the Park

THE DRAWING
1 Use canvas board or canvas, 14 inches by 18 inches vertically.
2 Study the drawing and painting on pages 28 and 29.
3 Arrange the palette according to the palette layout on page 9.
4 Prepare canvas as for the previous paintings, stained with umber wash and sectioned off.
5 Put in drawing, using grids for correct placement. Notice the different heights and shapes of the buildings. Leave the detail on the top of the buildings till last.
6 The light is coming from the left, so lightly shade buildings, etc., on the right.
7 Draw only the tree trunks for now. You can put in the branches later.
8 Clean your brushes in the medium.

THE PAINTING

SKY

Colour formula
Sky tones

light   medium   dark

Refer to page 15 for sky tones and mix according to the directions. Only the medium and light tones are used for the sky. The dark tone is to be used for the buildings.

Let's paint

1 Study the painting on page 29.
2 Paint the light sky tone around the buildings and half-way into the sky.
3 Starting at the top of the canvas, paint with medium tone and work into the light tone, taking care not to lose the light tone.

BUILDINGS
Keep them simple. They are just an impression.

1 Paint the buildings in the dark sky tone. Notice the detail at the top of them and put it in loosely.
2 Paint some medium sky tone into the left side of the buildings for form. The light is coming from the left. The blue tones push the buildings far into the background.

Lesson 4 continues on page 30

GREEN SLOPES

light   medium   dark

Refer to page 14 for tones of green and mix according to the directions.

1 Study the painting on the previous page. There are three slopes.
2 Paint the dark green tone on the right side of each slope down to the bushes.
3 Paint medium tone on the rest of each slope. Take care with your strokes.

SHRUBS ON SLOPES
1 Study the formation of shrubs carefully in the painting on the previous page. There are approximately three shrubs on each slope.
2 With a dabbling stroke, paint dark green tone on the right side of each shrub. Dabble some purple on this and under the shrub for a little shadow.
3 Dabble the medium green tone on the left side of the shrubs, taking care to maintain the form.
4 Highlight the shrubs by stroking on a little light sky tone on top of the medium green tone.

If you run out of green tones, mix another batch.

SHRUBS ALONG PATH
1 Study the painting on the previous page.
2 Paint the shrubs in the same way as the shrubs on the slopes with tones of green.

HIGHLIGHTS

1 Highlight the shrubs along path by dabbling the extra light yellow-green tone on top of the medium green tone on the left and across the front of the shrubs. Take care not to lose the medium green tone.

GRASS FOREGROUND
Keep the foreground dark for depth. Notice the light in the painting along the path.

1 Paint the dark green tone in front of the trees, using flowing strokes.
2 Highlight the path in front of trees with the extra light yellow-green tone.
3 Paint dark green tone up into the tree trunks a little way.

PATH
1 With yellow ochre from palette, paint path using a left to right short cross stroke.
2 Drag a little purple from under shrubs across the path to form shadows.

TREES

1 Study the painting on page 29. The branches evolve one from another in a downward curve.
2 Paint the tree trunks thickly with purple from palette.
3 Paint the branches with the palette knife if you can, but if this is too difficult use No. 6 round brush to draw in branches lightly where indicated in the painting. Do not make them too definite or draw too many, and take care to keep the character of the trees.
4 Paint in a few strokes of aqua on the trunks.

LEAVES

1 Study the painting on page 29. It is early spring, so there are relatively few leaves and these are pale green and painted across the branches.
2 Dabble some dark and medium green tones in upper part of the trees and a few leaves in the lower branches.
3 Dabble the extra light yellow-green tone in uneven lines across the branches, never up and down the branches.
4 Blend some dark green tone with the purple on the tree trunk, then work a little purple shadow in front of the trees.
5 With the knife scratch in a few blades of grass around the trunk in wet paint.

Clean palette, brushes and knives.

This is a satisfying painting and I'm sure it is getting easier. Keep painting.

Lesson 5
Pears

THE DRAWING

1 Use canvas board or canvas, 14 inches by 18 inches horizontally.
2 Study the drawing and painting on pages 34 and 35.
3 Arrange the palette according to the palette layout on page 9.
4 Prepare canvas as for the previous paintings, stained with umber wash and sectioned off.
5 Put in drawing, using grids for correct placement. Reduce the vase and bowl to squares first, then draw in forms. Be sure that the pears are lying in the bowl.
6 The light is coming from the right, so lightly shade in the left side of pears, vase and bowl.
7 Clean your brushes in the medium.

THE PAINTING

BACKGROUND

Colour formula
Tones of yellow ochre

light   medium   dark

Medium tone
1 tablespoon yellow ochre
½ teaspoon white
Mix and separate into three parts, one small (½ teaspoon) and two equal parts.
First part (½ teaspoon) for light tone
add   1 teaspoon white
½ teaspoon lemon yellow

Second part for medium tone: do not touch

Third part for dark tone
add   ½ teaspoon purple

Clean your knife.

Let's paint

1 Study the painting on page 35.
2 Paint in the background, starting with the dark tone on the left, the medium tone in the middle and the light tone on the right. Use long strokes made with the flat of the knife and blend tones lightly. Paint around the objects carefully.
3 Paint purple from palette under the objects to form shadows.
4 With the flat of the knife, lightly drag purple in downward strokes, then score the canvas horizontally over this to make reflections.

VASE

light   medium   dark

Mix and separate into three parts, one small (½ teaspoon) and two equal parts.

Clean your knife.

1 Study the painting on page 35.
2 Paint the left side of the vase with dark blue tone, using curved strokes and taking care to maintain the form.
3 Paint the middle of the vase with medium tone. Don't lose the opening at the top of the vase.
4 Paint the right side with light tone, using curved strokes in the shape of the vase.
5 With purple from palette, fill in the opening of the vase. Notice that the opening, the centre and bottom of the vase are all curved downward in the same direction.
6 Blend a little purple on left side and bottom of vase. (Add the highlights later.)
7 Paint some light blue tones in left side of background, as indicated in the painting.

BOWL

light   medium   dark

Refer to page 10 for tones of burnt orange and mix according to the directions.

1 Paint the left side of the bowl with the dark burnt orange tone. Curve strokes to the shape of the bowl. Remember that, as with the vase, the top and bottom of the bowl are curved downwards in the same direction.

2 Paint the middle of the bowl with medium tone.
3 Paint the right side of the bowl with the light tone.

PEARS

Colour formula
Tones of green

light   medium   dark

Refer to page 14 for tones of green and mix according to the directions.

1 Study the painting on the previous page and notice particularly the shape and position of the pears.
2 Paint dark green tone on the left side of all the pears. Notice the curved stroke on the cheek of the pears.
3 Paint medium tone in the middle of the pears, taking care not to lose the dark tone.
4 Paint light tone on the right side, using curved strokes to maintain the shape. Blend the colours slightly.
5 With purple from palette, paint around the inside, left side and bottom of the bowl.
6 Paint the pear lying down with curved strokes of dark, medium and light green tones as indicated in the painting. Add highlights later.
7 Paint some light blue tones on the left side of all the pears.
8 With purple from palette paint short, slender stems on the pears.

HIGHLIGHTS
For vase, bowl and pears.

Colour tone
$\frac{3}{4}$ teaspoon white
$\frac{1}{4}$ teaspoon Naples yellow

1 As in Still Life on page 23, paint a short blob of the above colour curved in the shape of the vase, bowl and pears, on the right side.

Clean palette, brushes and knives.

Another masterpiece, you will agree. And there is more to come.

Lesson 6
White on White - Carnations

THE DRAWING

1 Use canvas board or canvas, 14 inches by 18 inches vertically.
2 Study the drawing and painting on pages 38 and 39.
3 Arrange the palette according to the palette layout on page 9.
4 Prepare canvas as for the previous paintings, stained with umber wash and sectioned off.
5 Put in drawing, using grids for correct placement. Notice the pods under the heads of the flowers and the shape and angle of the circles. The flowers are either in profile or full on.
6 The light is coming from the right, so shade the areas on the left of the carnations.
7 Clean your brushes in the medium.

THE PAINTING

BACKGROUND

Colour formula
Tones of white

light   medium   dark

The procedure for mixing this colour is different from the previous methods.

Light tone
1¾ tablespoons white
⅛ teaspoon Naples yellow
Mix and separate into three equal parts.
First part for light tone: do not touch

Second part for medium tone
add   ⅛ teaspoon burnt umber
      ⅛ teaspoon aqua

Third part for dark tone
add   ¼ teaspoon burnt umber
      ¼ teaspoon aqua

Clean your knife.

Let's paint

1 Study the painting on page 39. It is a monochromatic painting, i.e. variations of the same tone. The glass vase will be painted in the same tones as the background.
2 Paint in the background, starting with the dark white tone on the left. Go through half of the vase with dark tone but leave the outline of the vase.
3 Paint medium tone in the middle of the canvas and through the other half of the vase, leaving the outline.

4 Paint the light tone on the right of the canvas, blending the tones lightly.
5 To make the dark tone for the area between the flowers and the outline of the vase and the shading, mix the following:

to $\frac{1}{2}$ **teaspoon dark white tone**
add $\frac{1}{4}$ **teaspoon purple**
$\frac{1}{8}$ **teaspoon yellow ochre**

6 Using the above mixture, paint between the flowers, taking care not to lose them, and go into the vase a little.
7 Paint the outline of the vase carefully with this same mixture, as indicated in the painting.
8 Using the flat of the knife, paint this same tone under the vase, dragging it down as in the Pears painting on page 35. Scratch a few horizontal strokes over it for reflection.

FLOWERS

**Colour formula
Tones of white**

light medium dark

Refer to page 37 for tones of white and mix according to the directions. These are the same tones as those used for the background.

1 Study the painting on the previous page.
2 Always start in the centre of the bouquet and work outwards. Practise strokes on paper before painting the flowers.
3 Paint dark tone on left and top of flowers. Simply press down knife to create a rather long, narrow, horizontal stroke. Alternate with medium tone, using the same stroke. Notice the narrow flowers' profile.
4 Paint the front and right side of the flowers with light tone, creating two or three petals on each flower.
5 When the flowers are all finished, scratch the edges of the petals with a clean knife to form the petal shape of carnations.

LEAVES

**Colour formula
Tones of green**

light medium dark

Refer to page 14 for tones of green and mix according to the directions. These same tones of green are also used for the pods, buds and stems.

1 Study the painting on page 39. The leaves are long, slender and spiky and there are not very many of them. Practise them on paper first.
2 Paint the leaves with dark tone and just tip them with light tone.

3 Pat just a few blobs of green tones between the flowers to give the impression of leaves.

PODS
1 Paint the dark green tone on the left side of the pods just under the heads of the flowers.
2 Paint the light tone on the right side of the pods, taking care to maintain the form.

BUDS
1 Paint buds where and as you see them (study the painting), using the same dark and light green tones.

STEMS
1 Paint stems in the vase with dark green tone, criss-crossing them as shown in the painting.
2 Paint the light tone on the bottom of the stems in the vase.
3 Paint a little purple on the stems going into the vase.
4 Use light green tone to paint the stems showing in the centre of the floral.

HIGHLIGHTS
1 Using the light white tone, paint highlights on the vase where indicated in the painting. Use curved strokes to maintain the shape.
2 Paint the fallen petals and a few leaves with the light white tone and put in a little purple underneath each, dragged down, to form shadow.
3 Paint a few strokes of aqua through the floral and on the left side and bottom of the vase.

Clean palette, brushes and knives.

I am sure you found this painting a real challenge — but you may find that it is your favourite.

Lesson 7
Early Morning

This is similar to Spring in the Park on page 29, in that only two colour formulas are used throughout the painting.

THE DRAWING
1 Use canvas board or canvas, 14 inches by 18 inches horizontally.
2 Study the drawing and painting on pages 44 and 45.
3 Arrange the palette according to the palette layout on page 9.
4 Prepare canvas as for the previous paintings, stained with umber wash and sectioned off.
5 Put in drawing, using grids for correct placement. Put in horizon first just a little below the centre line. The line of the mountains vary in shape and height and the mountains are reflected in the water.
6 The light is coming from the left, so shade the areas on the right.
7 Clean your brushes in the medium.

THE PAINTING

SKY

Colour formula
Sky tones

light   medium   dark

Refer to page 15 for sky tones and mix according to the directions. As in Spring in the Park on page 29, only the medium and light sky tones are used for the sky. The dark tone is used for the mountains.

Let's paint

1 Study the painting on page 45. The sky and mountain tones are repeated in the water for reflections.
2 Paint the light tone around the top of the mountains and half-way into the sky.
3 Starting at the top of the canvas, paint medium tone and work it into the light tone at a slight angle.
4 Clean your knife and use it to drag sky tone lightly into the mountains. This will soften the lines of the mountains, but take care not to lose the shape.
5 Repeat the sky tones in the water. Start with the light tone on the right, then the medium tone. Take care with the line of the mountains. Stroke straight across the canvas.

MOUNTAINS
1 Paint the right side of the mountains with dark sky tone.
2 Paint the left side with dark and medium sky tones together.
3 Paint a little purple from the palette lightly on the right side and base of the mountains.
4 Repeat the painting of the mountains in the water.

5 Paint a little purple from palette along the water's edge, crossways, to form shadows. Blend lightly.
6 Clean the knife and, with the tip, scratch lines vertically across the water in the wet paint, then horizontally. This creates reflections and blends tones.

GROUND

Colour formula
Tones of green

light   medium   dark

Refer to page 14 for tones of green and mix according to the directions.

1 Study the painting on page 45.
2 Paint the dark green tone in long strokes on the right side of the ground and bring it up to the bushes.
3 Paint medium tone and then light tone on the left. Blend all tones.
4 Paint the dark tone in the areas along the water's edge with short up and down strokes, using the flat of the knife. Paint purple and aqua from the palette over this very lightly.
5 Using the dark green tone, paint along the bottom of the canvas, in the foreground. Blend a little purple over this.
6 Paint light green tone in left-hand corner and blend with dark tone.
7 With clean knife, scratch grasses in wet paint along the foreground.

BUSHES
1 Study the painting on page 45. The bushes occur along the base of the mountains at different heights.
2 Using dabbling strokes, paint dark green tone and purple from palette on the right side and bottom of the bushes.
3 Paint medium green tone on the left side of the bushes.
4 Dabble light green tone on the left side of the bushes, keeping them uneven.

TREES
1 Study the painting on page 45.
2 Paint the tree trunks near the mountains with light sky tone. Keep them delicate.
3 Paint leaves going across the branches with dark and medium green tones on the right side and light green tone on the left side.
4 Paint the tree in the left foreground in purple. Notice the structure of the branches. Try to paint them with the knife but, if you find this too difficult, use the No. 6 round brush. Paint them in lightly and not too many.
5 Dabble dark and medium green tones for leaves across the top of the tree.
6 Paint the light tone on the top of the clumps of leaves.
7 Repeat the leaves where indicated in the painting, then dabble them with lemon yellow from palette. Keep them delicate and lacy.

Clean palette, brushes and knives.

Another masterpiece. By now you are flipping that knife like a professional and you will find each painting easier and more exciting.

Lesson 8
Snow Scene

THE DRAWING

1 Use canvas board or canvas, 14 inches by 18 inches horizontally.
2 Study the drawing and painting on pages 48 and 49.
3 Arrange the palette according to the palette layout on page 9.
4 Prepare the canvas as for the previous paintings, stained with umber wash and sectioned off.
5 Put in drawing, using grids for correct placement. Find the horizon line first. This one is one inch above the centre line. Contain the cottage in a square first before you draw it.
6 The light is coming from the right, so shade in the areas on the left. Note the shading on the cottage.
7 Clean your brushes in the medium.

THE PAINTING

SKY

Colour formula
Sky tones

light   medium   dark

Refer to page 15 for sky tones and mix according to the directions. Again, only the medium and light tones are used for the sky. The dark tone is used for the rocks, stream, etc.

Let's paint

1 Study the painting on page 49.
2 Paint light sky tone around cottage, along slopes, covering up the trees for now, and partly up into the sky.
3 With the medium sky tone, start painting at the top of the canvas and work down into the light tone, taking care not to lose the light tone. Blend lightly.

COTTAGE

Colour tone
**to each of ½ teaspoon medium sky tone and ½ teaspoon dark sky tone
add ¼ teaspoon yellow ochre**

1 Paint the left side of the cottage and the lean-to in the dark tone of the above mixture.
2 Paint the right side of the cottage and lean-to with the medium tone of the same mixture. Leave the roof for now and paint just a suggestion of window and door.

SNOW

light　　　medium　　　dark

Refer to page 37 for tones of white and mix according to the directions.

1 Study the painting on page 49.
2 Paint the dark and medium white tones on the left of the slope and around the rocks.
3 Paint light tone on the right of the slope.
4 Paint the slope behind the tree in medium and light tones, using long, flowing strokes.
5 Paint dark and medium tones across the bottom in the foreground and up into the large tree.
6 Paint light tone on right foreground and again up into the tree a little way.
7 Paint the roof on the left side of the cottage and lean-to in the medium tone.
8 Paint the front part of the roof with the light tone.
9 Paint the chimney on the top of the roof with dark white tone and the one in the front with a dab of vermilion from palette.

TREES ON THE SLOPE
1 Dabble the dark white tone in small, round clumps to give the impression of trees. Paint them behind the cottage as indicated in the painting.
2 Under these clumps, scratch in with dark white tone trunks and branches of different lengths to give just an impression.

ROCKS
1 Paint the left side of the rocks in dark sky tone, as indicated in the painting.
2 Paint purple from palette around the base of the rocks for shadows.
3 Paint the light white tone on the right side and over the top of the rocks.
4 Paint the medium white tone under the rocks.
5 Paint the light white tone for the rest of the stream, using strokes going straight across the canvas. Blend the tones lightly.
6 Paint purple from palette under the rocks in the water for shadows.
7 Paint in a few strokes of yellow ochre from palette in the stream to give highlights.
8 Clean the knife and scratch in vertical lines in the stream and then a few horizontal strokes.

LARGE TREE
1 Study the painting on page 49. This beautiful old tree dominates the painting.
2 Paint the trunk with purple from palette. Notice the texture of the trunk and paint with long, flowing strokes.
3 Paint the heavy branches with purple.
4 Paint the right side of the trunk with dark white tone, taking care with your strokes.
5 Blend the purple of the tree into the snow at the base.
6 Paint a few strokes of light white tone on the right side of the trunk.
7 Work a little aqua on the left side of the trunk and on the rocks.
8 Paint a few strokes of yellow ochre at the base and on the right side of the trunk.

Clean palette, brushes and knives.

You now have the experience of painting snow. This is a lovely, nostalgic painting.

Lesson 9
Pink Poppies

THE DRAWING
1 Use canvas board or canvas, 14 inches by 18 inches vertically.
2 Study the drawing and painting on pages 52 and 53.
3 Arrange the palette according to the palette layout on page 9.
4 Prepare the canvas as for previous paintings, stained with umber wash and sectioned off.
5 Put in the drawing, using grids for correct placement.
6 The light is coming from the left, so shade the areas on the right.
7 Clean your brushes in the medium.

THE PAINTING

BACKGROUND

Colour formula
Tones of blue-purple

light   medium   dark

Medium tone
1 tablespoon white
$\frac{1}{4}$ **teaspoon blue**
$\frac{1}{2}$ **teaspoon aqua**
$\frac{3}{4}$ **teaspoon orange**
$\frac{1}{4}$ **teaspoon purple**
$\frac{1}{8}$ **teaspoon alizarin crimson**

Mix and separate into three parts, one small ($\frac{1}{2}$ teaspoon) and two equal parts.
First part ($\frac{1}{2}$ teaspoon) for light tone
add   **1 teaspoon white**
$\frac{1}{4}$ **teaspoon alizarin crimson**

Second part for medium tone: do not touch

Third part for dark tone
add $\frac{1}{4}$ **teaspoon purple**
$\frac{1}{4}$ **teaspoon aqua**
$\frac{1}{4}$ **teaspoon orange**
$\frac{1}{8}$ **teaspoon alizarin crimson**

Clean your knife.

Let's paint

1 Study the painting on page 53.
2 Using the flat of the knife, paint in the background, starting with dark tone on the right, then medium tone in the middle and light tone on the left. Blend the tones lightly and go around the flowers loosely.
3 Paint purple from palette under the vase and on the lower right side of the canvas.

4 Paint purple in the centre of the bouquet between the flowers, taking care not to lose the shapes.
5 Clean your knife, then drag the purple under the vase downwards.
6 Score the purple with the tip of the knife horizontally to form shadows and reflections underneath the vase.

VASE

Colour formula
Tones of blue

light   medium   dark

Refer to page 33 for tones of blue and mix according to the directions.

1 Study the painting on page 53.
2 Paint the right side and bottom of the vase with dark tone.
3 Paint the middle of the vase with medium tone.
4 Paint the left side of the vase with light tone.
5 Under the flowers at the top of the vase paint purple and a little alizarin crimson for shadow. Blend tones lightly.
6 Outline the vase lightly with purple.

FLOWERS

Colour formula
Tones of pink

light   medium   dark

Medium tone
1 tablespoon white
⅛ teaspoon vermilion
½ teaspoon alizarin crimson
Mix and separate into three parts, one small (½ teaspoon) and two equal parts.
First part (½ teaspoon) for light tone
add   1 teaspoon white
½ teaspoon Naples yellow
touch of orange

Second part for medium tone: do not touch

Third part for dark tone
add   ½ teaspoon alizarin crimson
⅛ teaspoon purple

Clean your knife.

1 Study the drawing on page 52. One half of the flowers on the right are shaded at the top, the other half are shaded on the undersides of the flowers. Practise a few flowers on paper first.

2 Paint the shaded areas of the flowers on the right with fan-shaped strokes of dark tone.
3 Paint the medium tone on the remaining half of each flower on the right, again using fan-shaped strokes to form the petals.
4 With the tip of the knife, go around the underneaths of the flowers and where the tones meet around the top of the flowers.
5 Paint the top of the flowers on the left of the bouquet with fan-shaped strokes of light tone.
6 Paint the underneath part of each flower on the left with fan-shaped strokes of medium tone.
7 With the tip of the knife, round off the shape of the flowers.
8 Paint a little light tone on top of the medium tone on the flowers on the right.
9 Paint a little dark tone on top of the medium tone on the flowers on the left.
10 Paint a few fallen petals with light, medium and dark tones.
11 Put a few dots of purple from palette in the centre of each flower for stamens.

LEAVES

Colour formula
Tones of green

light   medium   dark

Refer to page 14 for tones of green and mix according to the directions.

1 Study the painting on the previous page. The green tones give just an impression of leaves and there are not very many. Practise a few on paper first.
2 Paint a few blobs of dark and medium green tones between the flowers on the right.
3 Paint a little light tone underneath the heads of the flowers to make tiny leaves.
4 Paint a few stems with light tone.
5 Paint a few blobs of light and medium tones between the flowers on the left side.
6 Paint a few sketchy leaves with light and dark tones near to the base of the bouquet, coming out of the bouquet on the left and at the top.
7 Paint a few buds with light and dark tones as indicated in the painting.
8 Paint a few sketchy leaves with medium and light tones on the right side, again coming out of the bouquet between the flowers.
9 Paint a couple of fallen leaves on the left and paint purple underneath them, dragging the colour down for shadow.

HIGHLIGHTS

Colour tone
to $\frac{1}{4}$ **teaspoon light blue tone (used for the vase)**
add $\frac{1}{4}$ **teaspoon white**
touch of Naples yellow

1 Paint a blob of the above colour on the vase in a curved stroke.
2 Lightly paint in strokes of aqua on the vase and bouquet, as indicated in the painting. Add a few downward strokes of aqua under the vase.

Clean palette, brushes and knives.

By now I expect the procedure is becoming a little more automatic and you will be able to concentrate more on your subject.

Lesson 10
Low Tide

THE DRAWING

1 Use canvas board or canvas, 14 inches by 18 inches horizontally.
2 Study the drawing and painting on pages 56 and 57.
3 Arrange the palette according to the palette layout on page 9.
4 Prepare the canvas as for previous paintings, stained with umber wash and sectioned off.
5 Put in the drawing, using grids for correct placement. For the little boat, draw a long, narrow box first, then draw the boat within that area. Check your horizon in this painting. It falls a little above the centre line.
6 The light is coming from the right, so shade in the areas on the left.
7 Clean your brushes in the medium.

THE PAINTING

SKY

Colour formula
Sky tones

light   medium   dark

Refer to page 15 for sky tones and mix according to the directions.

Let's paint

1 Study the painting on page 57.
2 Paint around the top of the hills and up into the sky a little way with light tone.
3 Starting at the top of the canvas, paint medium tone in downward strokes. Blend it with the light tone, taking care not to lose the light tone.
4 Paint a vague impression of mountains at the back of the hills with dark tone, blending with the sky colour.
5 Clean your knife.

YELLOW HILLS

Colour formula
Tones of yellow ochre

light   medium   dark

Refer to page 32 for tones of yellow ochre and mix according to the directions.

1 Study the painting on page 57.
2 Paint the hill on the extreme right with light tone on the right of it and medium tone on the left of it.

3 Paint the hill next to it with light tone on the right of it and dark tone on the left of it.
4 Blend a little medium sky tone into the hills to tone down the yellow, taking care not to lose the shape of the hills.

GREEN HILLS

Colour formula
Tones of green

light   medium   dark

Refer to page 14 for tones of green and mix according to the directions.

1 Study the painting on the previous page.
2 Paint the remaining hills with light tone on the right and medium tone on the left.
3 Paint a bit of medium sky tone on top of the two green tones to tone the hills down a little and put them into the distance.
4 On the mound where the trees are, paint light green tone and a little yellow ochre from palette. Paint a little dark tone around the water's edge.
5 Paint in a few strokes of orange on the mound and the hills.

TREES
1 Using stippling strokes, paint medium green tone on the right side of the trees and dark green tone on the left side.
2 Stipple a tiny bit of light green tone over the medium tone.
3 With purple from palette, paint slender tree trunks and highlight them with a little light sky tone.

WATER
1 Study the painting on the previous page. As for Early Morning on page 45, the sky tones are also used for the water.
2 With light sky tone, paint the right side of the water to the middle of the canvas, taking care to preserve the shape of the inlets.
3 Continue with light sky tone along the shoreline at the base of all the hills.
4 Paint the medium tone next, shading to the dark tone on the left side of the water.
5 Paint the dark green tone straight down in the water on the left to make the reflection of the trees.
6 Paint the little inlets below the boat with light sky tone.
7 Paint a few strokes of light sky tone in the dark side to give the water sparkle.
8 With a clean knife, scratch vertical strokes and then horizontal strokes the length of the body of the water, to form reflections.

FOREGROUND
1 Study the painting on the previous page. The foreground slopes to the left and is painted in dark, cool, green tones.
2 Paint medium green tone on the right side of the canvas under the bushes, shading to dark green tone in the right-hand corner.
3 With purple from palette, paint short up and down strokes for vegetation under the bushes and around the boat.
4 Add a few strokes of orange from palette in the right-hand corner.
5 Paint the bottom edge of the canvas with dark green tone and a little purple.
6 Paint medium green tone up to the water's edge on the left side. Blend a little vermilion over this.

7 Paint a little dark sky tone over the ground below the bushes, then blend all the tones.
8 Paint the bushes on the right of the foreground with dark green tone and purple, shading to medium green tone. Use an up and down stroke.
9 Paint the ground below the hills with dark green tone, then blend in some dark sky tone.

BOAT
1 Study the painting on page 57. Use the No. 6 brush if the knife is too awkward.
2 Paint the inside of the boat with purple.
3 Paint the outside of the boat with dark yellow ochre tone.
4 Outline the boat with purple, blending the colours together.
5 Highlight the left side of the boat with a few strokes of light yellow ochre tone.
6 Clean your knife, then scratch in the mast of the boat.
7 Drag a line with the knife from the boat to the ground and highlight it with a few strokes of light yellow ochre tone.

Clean palette, brushes and knives.

This painting was a little more sophisticated but I'm sure you were able to cope with it. If you are not happy with the boat, just scrape it off with your knife.

Lesson 11
Violets

THE DRAWING
1 Use canvas board or canvas, 14 inches by 18 inches horizontally.
2 Study the drawing and painting on pages 60 and 61.
3 Arrange the palette according to the palette layout on page 9.
4 Prepare canvas as for previous paintings, stained with umber wash and sectioned off.
5 Put in the drawing, using grids for correct placement. Very little detail is needed in this drawing.
6 The light is coming from the left, so shade the areas on the right. Notice that the shading is in masses and around the edge of the flowers over the bowl, giving depth to the bouquet.
7 Clean your brushes in the medium.

THE PAINTING

BACKGROUND

Colour formula
Sky tones

light   medium   dark

Refer to page 15 for sky tones and mix according to the directions.

Let's paint

1 Study the painting on the previous page.
2 Using long strokes and the flat of the knife, paint dark tone on the right side of the canvas.
3 Paint medium tone in the middle.
4 Paint light tone on the left side of the canvas, lightly blending all tones.
5 Paint purple from palette under the bowl and on the right side of the canvas.
6 Using the flat of the knife, lightly drag strokes of purple downwards, then scratch a few horizontal strokes over for shadows and reflections.

BOWL

Colour formula
Tones of blue

light   medium   dark

Refer to page 33 for tones of blue and mix according to the directions.

1 Paint the right side and bottom of the bowl with dark tone, using round strokes.
2 Paint the middle of the bowl with medium tone.
3 Paint the left side of the bowl with light tone, then blend the tones lightly.

FLOWERS

Colour formula
Tones of purple

light   medium   dark

Medium tone
1 tablespoon white
$\frac{3}{4}$ teaspoon purple
$\frac{1}{8}$ teaspoon alizarin crimson

Mix and separate into three parts, one small ($\frac{1}{2}$ teaspoon) and two equal parts.

First part ($\frac{1}{2}$ teaspoon) for light tone
add 1 teaspoon white
$\frac{1}{8}$ teaspoon Naples yellow
touch of alizarin crimson

Second part for medium tone: do not touch

Third part for dark tone
add $\frac{3}{4}$ teaspoon purple
touch of alizarin crimson

For extra light tone, remove $\frac{1}{2}$ teaspoon light tone
add $\frac{1}{2}$ teaspoon white
touch of alizarin crimson
touch of Naples yellow

Clean your knife.

1 Study the painting on page 61 and practise a few violets on paper first. Each violet is made up of three blobs of purple tone.
2 For the flowers on the right side, paint two blobs of dark tone and one blob of medium tone.
3 For the flowers on the left side, paint two blobs of light tone and one blob of medium tone.
4 Paint across the bottom of the bouquet and along the bowl with dark and medium tones, in an uneven line, for shadow.
5 Paint a few blobs of light tone on the right side and some more in the centre of the bouquet.
6 Paint extra light purple tone on the left side of the violets.
7 Paint the single violets on the left and top of the bouquet in medium, light and extra light tones.
8 Paint the single violets on the right and top of the bouquet in light, medium and dark tones.
9 Paint the dropped flowers and petals with all the purple tones, as indicated in the painting.
10 Stroke some medium purple tone into the right side and left corner of the canvas, using flat strokes.
11 Paint dots of yellow ochre in the right side of the bouquet for flower centres.
12 Paint dots of cadmium yellow deep in the left side of the bouquet for flower centres.

LEAVES

Colour formula
Tones of green

light   medium   dark

Refer to page 14 for tones of green and mix according to the directions.

1 Study the painting on page 61. The leaves are tucked up under the violets.
2 Draw in the distinctive heart-shaped leaves where indicated in the painting using the No. 6 round brush and the medium and dark green tones.
3 Put a line down the centre of each leaf, using the dark tone.
4 Paint dark green tone and purple from palette on the top of all the leaves to make shadows from the violets.
5 Paint dark and medium green tones mostly on the right side of the leaves.
6 Paint light tone on the left side of the leaves and where indicated in the painting.
7 Paint dropped leaves in dark, medium and light green tones.

HIGHLIGHTS
1 Paint a curved stroke of light sky tone on the left side of the bowl.

Clean palette, brushes and knives.

It took a bit of doing to make those blobs look like violets, I'm sure.

Lesson 12
Wooded Glen

THE DRAWING

1　Use canvas board or canvas, 14 inches by 18 inches horizontally.
2　Study the drawing and painting on pages 66 and 67.
3　Arrange the palette according to the palette layout on page 9.
4　Prepare canvas as for previous paintings, stained with umber wash and sectioned off.
5　Put in the drawing, using grids for correct placement. Remember, the horizon line is not in the centre. In this painting it is below the centre which means that either the top or the bottom of your painting is dominant. In this one, it is the top part.
6　The light is coming from the right, so shade the areas on the left.
7　Clean your brushes in the medium.

THE PAINTING

SKY

Colour formula
Sky tones

light　　　medium　　　dark

Refer to page 15 for sky tones and mix according to the directions.

Let's paint

1　Study the painting on page 67.
2　Paint along the horizon with dark sky tone, spreading it upwards into the sky. Take care not to cover up the tree trunks on the left of the painting.
3　Paint the middle of the sky with light tone.
4　Paint the top of the canvas with dark tone, then blend all the tones lightly.

GREEN TREES

Colour formula
Tones of green

light　　　medium　　　dark

Refer to page 14 for tones of green and mix according to the directions. The greens in this painting are cool, so mix the following tones:

A　to $\frac{1}{2}$ teaspoon medium green tone
　　add　$\frac{1}{2}$ teaspoon medium sky tone

B　to $\frac{1}{2}$ teaspoon of the above mixture
　　add　$\frac{1}{2}$ teaspoon dark green tone

1 Study the painting on page 67. The colours of the trees are hazy and cool.
2 Paint the pale green trees with green tone A, using dabbling strokes.
3 Paint the small tree on the right with green tone B.
4 Add a few strokes of purple from palette in the centre and at the bottom of the leaves.

GREEN GRASS

Extra light green tone
to original light green tone
add ½ teaspoon white

1 Paint along the horizon with the above colour as indicated in the painting.
2 Paint dark green tone under the trees for shadows.

TREE TRUNKS

1 Study the painting on page 67.
2 For the tree trunks on the left of the painting, paint purple from palette on the left of trunk and dark sky tone on the right.
3 Paint the large branches with purple from palette.
4 Paint the slender trunks in the centre and along the horizon with purple.

BURNT ORANGE TREES

Colour formula
Tones of burnt orange

light   medium   dark

Refer to page 10 for tones of burnt orange and mix according to the directions.

1 Study the painting on page 67 and keep the trees small.
2 Using dabbling strokes, paint the trees in layers of alternate tones, starting with dark tone for the leaves at the base, then medium tone above and light tone above that.
3 Repeat until you have completed the shape of the trees, making the foliage fuller near the base.
4 Dabble a few strokes of cadmium orange deep from palette on top of the light tone.
5 With purple from palette paint in a few branches from the trunks up into the leaves.

YELLOW LEAVES

Colour formula
Tones of yellow ochre

light   medium   dark

Refer to page 32 for tones of yellow ochre and mix according to the directions.

1 Study the painting on page 67.
2 Dabble dark yellow ochre and burnt orange tones on the left.
3 Dabble the same tones across the top of the canvas but keep them light as the sky must show through the leaves.

4 Dabble medium yellow ochre tone on top of the dark tone and on the right of the tree trunks.
5 Dabble a few light yellow ochre tones among the leaves, as shown in the painting.

GROUND, PATH
1 Study the painting on the previous page and notice particularly the shadows.
2 Paint light yellow ochre tone on the tiny area along the horizon for bright sunlight.
3 Paint the shadows, using stippling strokes, alternately with dark burnt orange tones, yellow ochre and purple from palette.
4 Blend the purple of the trees into the shadows on the path.
5 Paint the foreground with the same tones as for the shadows, taking care to maintain the angle of the shadows.
6 With stippling stroke, paint area between the shadows in the medium and dark yellow ochre tones.
7 Stipple light yellow ochre tone on top of the above colour tones, on the ground below the small tree and along the rut in the path in the foreground.
8 Paint light strokes of dark sky tone in the foreground.

Clean palette, brushes and knives.

This is a particularly vibrant painting and now you will have paintings of all the seasons in this series.

Lesson 13
Geraniums

THE DRAWING
1 Use canvas board or canvas, 14 inches by 18 inches vertically.
2 Study the drawing and painting on pages 70 and 71.
3 Arrange the palette according to the palette layout on page 9.
4 Prepare the canvas as for previous paintings, stained with umber wash and sectioned off.
5 Put in the drawing, using grids for correct placement. Notice that the flower pot is to one side.
6 The light is coming from the right, so shade the areas on the left.
7 Clean your brushes in the medium.

THE PAINTING

BACKGROUND

Colour formula
Tones of yellow ochre

light   medium   dark

Refer to page 32 for tones of yellow ochre and mix according to the directions.

Let's paint

1 Study the painting on page 71.
2 With long, flowing strokes, paint dark tone on the left of the canvas. Go around the flowers loosely.
3 Paint the medium tone in the middle of the canvas.
4 Paint light tone on the right of the canvas, again using long, flowing strokes.
5 With purple paint the lower left side of the canvas and around the bottom of the pot.
6 Drag purple strokes downwards under the pot, then scratch in a few horizontal strokes over them for shadows and reflections.

FLOWER POT

Colour formula
Tones of burnt orange

light   medium   dark

Refer to page 10 for tones of burnt orange and mix according to the directions.

1 Paint dark tone on the left side and base of the pot. Add some dark tone to top of the pot to form shadows from the flowers.
2 Paint medium tone in the middle of the pot and below the shadow at the top of the pot.
3 Paint light tone on the right side of the pot.
4 Paint in a few strokes of purple from palette on the left side of the pot and in among the base of the bouquet.

FLOWERS

Colours
Tones of red

cadmium orange deep   vermilion   alizarin crimson

light   medium   dark

The above colours are used from the palette and require no mixing. However, you will also need an extra light tone which you mix in the following way:

to each of $\frac{1}{2}$ teaspoon orange and $\frac{1}{8}$ teaspoon vermilion
add $\frac{3}{4}$ teaspoon white

1 Using dabbling strokes, paint alizarin crimson on the left side of the flowers, taking care to maintain the shape. The flowers at the top are in profile and are therefore a narrow shape. Some are almost in bud form.
2 Dabble some cadmium orange deep and vermilion in the middle of each flower.
3 Dabble extra light tone on the right side. Do not paint the strokes too solid but allow some petals to show protruding.
4 Paint fallen petals with vermilion and paint purple underneath them for shadows.
5 With the flat of the knife, paint a few strokes of cadmium orange deep on the right of the background.

STEMS

light   medium   dark

Refer to page 14 for tones of green and mix according to the directions.

1 Paint about four short stems underneath each flower's head in medium tone. Remember the head of a geranium is made up of several small blooms, each with its own stem.
2 Attach these short stems to main stems drawn, with medium tone, down into the pot where indicated in the painting. Be sure that the stems go into the pot naturally from the flowers on the right.
3 With light tone, paint a few small buds hanging between these short stems and tip them with vermilion.

LEAVES

1 Study the painting on the previous page. The leaves are slightly heart-shaped but mostly the colour is used to give just an impression of leaves.
2 Paint leaves on the left side and between the flowers with dark green tone, edging them with medium tone.
3 Paint the leaves in front dark tone on the right side and light tone on the left side.
4 Paint the leaves on the right side mostly light tone with dark tone at the base of the leaves.
5 Add a few strokes of lemon yellow from palette to the leaves, as indicated in the painting.
6 Paint a few dropped leaves with light, medium and dark tones. Paint purple underneath them for shadows.
7 Paint a few strokes of aqua in the floral.

Clean palette, brushes and knives.

You have just finished your painting course with paintings that you not only enjoyed doing but that you can be proud of.

You will not have learnt everything there is to know about painting — that comes with experience. But this methodical approach to painting and the colour formulas will be your launching pad into doing your own thing. My ten years of teaching students from all over the world have proved that.

Naturally your paintings will not look exactly like those in the book. They are not supposed to. But they will be good paintings and your own creative interpretation, and that's what it's all about.